ILLUSTRATED TALES OF
DERBYSHIRE

DAVID PAUL

AMBERLEY

Acknowledgements

Many people have assisted me during my research for this book, helping to focus my attention when delving into the customs, traditions and folklore relating to the county. It would be invidious not to mention at the outset numberless staff in many of the county's libraries who furnished me with many documents relating to the county's history. More importantly perhaps, for giving so freely of their time I would wish to record my heartfelt thanks. I would also wish to thank and acknowledge the generous assistance given to me by Erica Hague of Dronfield for sharing with me her extensive knowledge of Dronfield Grammar School and the history of Dronfield in general. Similarly, I must acknowledge the help given to me by John Wilton of Matlock who spent some considerable time explaining to me the intricate details relating to the murder of Dr Cuddie. A word of thanks must also be extended to Philippa Ainsworth for sharing with me her extensive knowledge of well dressing in Derbyshire.

There are many other people to whom I owe a debt of thanks, but it would be remiss of me not to record my thanks to my wife, Janet, for accompanying me when taking photographs of the various locations mentioned in the text, and also to my son, Jon, who read and made a number of corrections to the manuscript.

With reference to some of the black and white images included in the text, I would wish to state that despite prolonged and exhaustive enquiries, tracking down some copyright holders has not been possible.

Finally, whilst I have tried to ensure that the information in the text is factually correct, any errors or inaccuracies are mine alone.

First published 2020

Amberley Publishing
The Hill, Stroud
Gloucestershire, GL5 4EP

www.amberley-books.com

Copyright © David Paul, 2020

The right of David Paul to be identified as the Author
of this work has been asserted in accordance with the
Copyrights, Designs and Patents Act 1988.

British Library Cataloguing in Publication Data.
A catalogue record for this book is available from the British Library.

ISBN 978 1 4456 9511 2 (paperback)
ISBN 978 1 4456 9512 9 (ebook)

Typesetting by Aura Technology and Software Services, India.
Printed in Great Britain.

Contents

Introduction

Derbyshire is often characterised by rolling hills, picturesque villages, breathtaking views and lively market towns, stretching from the High Peak in the north of the county to the southern Pennines in the south. It is therefore very easy to understand why the county presents a melange of age-old traditions and customs, popular folk stories and tales of social significance. The history of the Pentrich Rising is one such event, when, at the beginning of the nineteenth century, a group of well-intentioned and dedicated men tried, against the odds, to bring about social equality in the country; they were rewarded with hanging, deportation and custodial prison sentences. On a more whimsical note is the tale of the man who stole the parson's sheep. Although, ostensibly, about stealing a sheep, the story ends with the parson's parishioners finding out that the good parson was as susceptible as his parishioners to the weaknesses of the flesh!

Another age-old tradition in Derbyshire is the custom of 'well dressing'. In fact, it must be one of the most famous, if not *the* most famous tradition still observed throughout the county. The custom was originally thought to have been a pagan rite held in honour of the nymphs, and corresponded with the ancient Roman Fontinalia, or annual flower festival of the spirits of the streams and fountains. The practice has since been adapted to Christian usage. Derbyshire is now widely acknowledged to be the home of 'well dressing'.

It is hoped that the stories that follow may preserve, in some small way, a few of the legends, folklore and traditions which help bestow upon Derbyshire such a rich heritage. The book does not purport, in any way, to be an academic text, but is aimed at the general reader.

David Paul
26 April 2019

The Bakewell Witches

It was known that Mrs Stafford, a milliner of Bakewell, lived with her sister, or possibly a friend, and, in order to make ends meet, she also took in lodgers. At one time she had an itinerant Scotsman as a lodger, but she had to evict him as he couldn't pay his rent. She threw him out onto the streets late one night, leaving him destitute without any of his clothes or other belongings.

Many months later he was found in a totally dishevelled state in a rat-infested cellar in London. He was brought before the magistrate on a charge of felonious intent, but, during his trial, he related the most remarkable account of the events leading up to his arrest. He informed the magistrates that one morning, whilst it was still dark, he was lying awake contemplating the day ahead. As he looked down, he could see through the clefts of the bedroom floor rays of bright light. He then observed his landlady sitting with another lady sat next to her, both of whom were dressed in outdoor clothes. He got out of bed and knelt down in order to see exactly what was going on in the room below. Next, he heard Mrs Stafford incanting some very strange words; words which sounded to him more like a spell:

> Over thick, over thin,
> Now, devil, to the cellar in Lunnun,

Five-arch bridge, Bakewell.

Site of the old
Town Hall,
Bakewell.

Then, all of a sudden, everything went dark again, and the house fell silent. It was
also obvious that the two women had gone. Totally bemused by the events that
he had just witnessed, he pondered as to what he should do next. He decided to
repeat the words himself, but his memory rendered:

> Through thick, through thin,
> Now, devil, to the cellar in Lunnun.

Immediately upon using the word 'through' instead of 'over', he was caught up in
an almighty hurricane which swept him away, still dressed in his sleeping clothes.
The next thing that he knew, he was sat side by side with the two witches, for
that was what he believed they were. He said that he'd noticed they were engaged
in wrapping up parcels containing silks and other fine materials, which they'd no
doubt stolen on their journey. The next thing he knew was that Mrs Stafford, who
was sat next to him, was offering him some wine. He fell unconscious immediately
upon drinking it. As soon as he regained consciousness, he found that he was sat
alone in a cold, rat-infested cellar. Just a few minutes later he was found by the
nightwatchman and taken to the magistrates. He was asked how he had arrived in
London with so few clothes. He couldn't give much of an answer, as he hadn't even
realised that he was in London, but he did say that most of his clothes should still be
at Bakewell. The judge found this difficult to believe, but he did order that the house
at Bakewell should be searched before he took any further action. As soon as his
wishes were carried out, the clothes were found just as the Scotsman had said! This
proved, beyond any reasonable doubt, that the two women were, in fact, witches.
The judge immediately gave orders for the information to be communicated to
magistrates in Derbyshire. When the information was duly received in Bakewell,
the two women were found, tried and executed at Derby.

Location: DE1 1NN

Above: All Saints' Parish Church, Bakewell.

Below: Almshouses, Bakewell.

The Blacksmith Who Sold Himself to the Devil

The story is told of a blacksmith from Calver who could not afford either coals or iron for his forge. He became totally despondent and could often be seen stamping around his foundry, shouting and swearing in a fit of rage and dejection. Then, one day when he was feeling very dispirited, a strange man, dressed all in black, appeared and said to the blacksmith, 'What dost thou want?' With a withering look, the blacksmith merely said that he wanted coal and iron for his fire. Surprisingly, the man in black then said to the blacksmith, 'If thou wilt sell thyself to me thou shalt want nought for seven years.' The blacksmith readily agreed to sell himself and, as soon as he returned to the forge, he found

Calver Methodist Church.

Early morning in Calver.

there was as much coal and iron as he needed to keep him in work for the next seven years. The blacksmith couldn't believe his luck, as it meant that he could provide for his wife and family for the foreseeable future. The blacksmith worked very happily for the next seven years, ensuring that his wife and family enjoyed a good standard of living, but then, at the end of the seven years the man in black returned. By this time, the blacksmith had realised that the man in black was indeed the devil himself. Meanwhile, the devil caused a great hole to appear in the blacksmith's field. He then had a bridge-type structure constructed over the hole, with the intention of enticing the blacksmith to walk over it, then fall into the hole and break his neck. The blacksmith was aware of why the devil wanted him to walk over the bridge and resolutely refused to do so. Furthermore, he turned to the devil and said, 'I won't. Take all thy coal and iron back to hell with thee.' Without more ado, the devil departed, leaving the blacksmith as poor as he had found him seven years previously.

Returning from his field, the blacksmith found that all of his coal and iron had disappeared, but he vowed that, rather than do any more of the devil's work, he would rather try to make an honest living as best as he could.

Location: S32 3XR

The Carter from Bubnell

Even the Duke of Devonshire at Chatsworth was not immune to worrying about the effects of the visitation of the plague at Eyam. A carter from Bubnell near to Baslow was plying his normal trade, and because there was a shortage of wood in the area, he'd been asked to deliver a load from the Earl of Devonshire's estate at Chatsworth to some of the nearby villages. But, as his route passed through Eyam, nobody from the village would accompany him on his foolhardy mission. Indeed, his family and neighbours, aware of the potentially hazardous journey he was contemplating, remonstrated with him and implored him not to venture anywhere near to Eyam. But the carter, being a physically strong man and in need of the money, chose to ignore their arguments and exhortations, and set off towards Chatsworth. Being alone, it took some time to load the cart, and, when he eventually did reach his final destination, the unloading took even longer, since none could be coaxed or cajoled into assisting him, in part because of the route he'd taken back from Chatsworth, but also because of the torrential rain that was now falling.

Bubnell Bridge.

River Derwent
at Bubnell.

Once his arduous day's work had been completed, the weary carter returned home in his wet clothes. Shortly afterwards he showed symptoms of a chill and developed a slight fever. He took to his bed. When news of the illness spread throughout the village, it was immediately construed as evidence that the carter had taken infection from the plague, thus spreading fear and alarm. His neighbours took decisive action, posting a vigilante guard outside of his cottage with strict instructions to raise the alarm should the carter attempt to cross the threshold. It was even rumoured that in this unlikely event occurring, the guard had permission to shoot him!

News of the carter's condition was also conveyed to the earl. When he was acquainted with details of the case, and wishing to allay fears, he instructed the messengers to return to their village, stating that his personal physician would visit the village on the morrow so that a thorough examination of the woebegone individual could take place. No doubt there was a secondary motive, in that the earl needed to reassure himself of his own continuing security – after all, Bubnell was less than 3 miles from Chatsworth, and, if there was any prospect of the plague spreading any nearer, then, clearly, it would be time for him and his family to depart and move out of harm's way.

Having been given explicit instructions by the earl, the doctor was hardly in any position to refuse, although he did exhibit a marked and understandable reluctance to visit any village in the near vicinity of Eyam. The following day he duly arrived in the village, but, being fearful of his own mortality, he sent instructions to the carter to leave his house and walk through the village until reaching the bridge that crossed the Derwent. He was then to cross the bridge and continue walking along the riverbank. But rather than follow the hapless carter across, the doctor stationed himself on the eastern bank! Then, by shouting a series of questions across the fast-flowing river, he was able to ascertain that the now suitably chastened and cowed carter was suffering from nothing more than a very heavy cold. He was given a prescription and, following a complete recovery, was duly, but reluctantly, released from the village-imposed quarantine.

Location: DE45 1PN

Lent and Collop Monday

The day before Shrove Tuesday was always referred to as Collop Monday in Derbyshire. It was the day when poorer people called on their richer neighbours to beg a collop of bacon to make fat for frying pancakes on the following day.

There was a bell called 'the Pancake Bell' at Dronfield Grammar School. On the morning of Shrove Tuesday the bell was rung for half an hour, after which time the boys were given a holiday. It was traditional for children in this parish to walk to the church carrying large open baskets to catch the pancakes, which were tossed over the church steeple on that day.

In the neighbouring parish of Eyam, the boys in the village rose as early as one or two o'clock on the morning of Shrove Tuesday and blew cow-horns, rattled old cans, and made a great uproar. Then, for some reason, the boy who remained longest in bed on that morning was called 'the bed churn'.

On Easter Sunday at Bradwell, children walked around the village dropping pins into various wells. It was the belief that a fairy presided over each well, and knew whether a child had deposited a pin in her well or not. Then, on the following Monday every child carried a bottle with them filled with sweetmeats,

Grounds of Henry Fanshawe School.

Henry Fanshawe School, formerly Dronfield Grammar School.

younger children having their bottles tied round their necks. It was said that the bottles of those children who had not dropped a pin into one of the wells would break, the fairy of the well-being the protector of the bottle. There were four or five wells in the village, one of them being in a place called 'Daniel's Garden'. After visiting all of the wells, the children went around to every house begging for a present of sugar.

The Church forbade the solemnisation of marriage ceremonies throughout the season of Lent.

In the neighbourhood of Dronfield and Eyam, Easter Monday was known in as 'Unlousing Day', or 'Lousing Day'. On that day it was the custom for men to lift and kiss young maidens. In the neighbouring Hathersage a young man was fined for kissing a young woman on that day. The practice of unlousing was also known at Baslow and at Bamford. At Bradwell, if a young man met a young woman on that day and stole a kiss he was said to have 'unloused' her. In that village the day was known as 'Lousing Day'.

It seems that kissing, as well as marrying, was considered to be unlawful during Lent, but after that time when Easter came, the sexes were set free – unloused – to marry.

Location: S18 1QB

The Little Red Hairy Man

There was once an old lead miner who lived in Wensley together with his three sons. One day the eldest son decided to try to make his mark. He packed his few belongings, made himself a sandwich and set off. He walked for quite a while, passing through a wood, but when he became tired he stopped, sat down and ate his bread and cheese. As he was eating, he caught sight of a little red man who had suddenly appeared from out of the wood. The little man approached the miner's son and asked him for something to eat, but instead of giving him food, the eldest son told him to 'get lost', and the little man went back into the wood.

Time passed and, ultimately, the eldest son returned home, but he was no better off than the day he left. Thinking that he might be able to do a little better, the second son decided to try his luck. After some deliberation, he set off and, coming to the wood, decided that it was time for a break. He sat down and began to eat his cheese and bread. When he was halfway through, the little red man whom his elder brother had seen appeared once again. He asked for something to eat, but the brother merely offered him the meagre remains of his lunch. In return, the little red man then suggested to the brother that it might be to his advantage if he went into the centre of the wood and looked for a particular mine that he would find there. The brother thought about what he had been told, but decided not to follow the advice. Instead, he returned home, not being any richer than the day he had left the village.

The youngest son, Jack, then decided to try his luck, and set off to seek his fortune. When he had travelled some way, he came to the wood and decided to stop and eat his lunch. Halfway through the little red man appeared. He said that he was hungry, so Jack cut him some of his bread and a huge piece of cheese. They ate their lunch together, and when they'd finished the little man turned to Jack and said, 'And now, I will help thee to get thy fortune, but thou must do as

Countryside around the village of Wensley.

Above: Main Street, Wensley.

Left: Wensley Reading Room.

I tell thee.' He then explained to Jack exactly how he could get to the mine. When they arrived at the mine Jack saw a deep shaft going down to it. He got into the shaft bucket and the little man wound him down until he got to the bottom where he found himself in what could only be described as a beautiful country. As Jack looked around he saw that the little old man was stood next to him holding a sword and a suit of armour, which he promptly gave to him. He then threw the copper ball that he had been holding onto to the ground and instructed Jack to follow it until it stopped. The ball rolled all the way to the copper castle, whereupon it flew against the door. A giant opened the door and immediately started to fight with Jack, but Jack's sword prevailed and the giant was killed. Jack set the princess free, and she was able to return to her own home. As Jack was walking back the old man caught up with him again. He told him that there was another princess being held captive, and that she must also be rescued. When Jack agreed to try to rescue the princess, the little man produced a silver ball, which he threw down, telling Jack to follow it as before. After some time the ball threw itself against a silver door, and the door was opened by a giant. And, as was also the case previously, the giant started to fight with Jack as soon as he opened the door, but Jack killed him with his sword and set the young princess free.

Jack found it hard to accept that there was a third princess whom the little man wanted him to rescue, but, once again, he agreed to try. This time the little old man produced a ball of pure gold for Jack to follow. When he reached the golden castle a giant opened the door, and started to fight. Jack killed him and rescued the princess, but, rather than her returning to her own home, Jack persuaded her to marry him. The little old man married them, and then helped Jack and his new wife to take as much gold as they could carry out of the mine before returning to Wensley.

Location: DE4 2LJ

Murder at Winnats Pass

The story of the murders on Winnats Pass near Castleton is thought to have taken place sometime in April 1758, when two eloping lovers, Allan and Clara (recorded as Henry and Clara in some accounts), were robbed and murdered by local lead miners.

Allan and Clara were eloping to Peak Forest Chapel, commonly known as the 'Gretna Green of England'. Allan came from a poorer family than Clara, and both of their families strongly disapproved of their relationship. At one point, which in some respects precipitated their elopement, Clara's brother became very abusive and threatening towards Allan.

The Peak Forest Chapel, built by Christian, Countess of Devonshire in 1657, and dedicated to Charles, King and Martyr, had been specifically chosen because of an anomalous legal situation whereby it was possible to become married in the chapel without necessarily fulfilling all of the normal requirements. However, Clara and Allan were not destined to marry at Peak Forest.

Before reaching their intended destination, they'd stayed at the Royal Oak in Stoney Middleton, aiming to complete their journey the following day. It was whilst they were there that they came into contact with a group of five drunken miners. Mistakenly, when seeing the couple dressed in fine clothes, the miners thought that they were a well-to-do rich couple. Plans were made to follow them whenever they continued on their journey. When the couple set off again, the miners followed them at a discreet distance. Then, as Clara and Allan were riding through Winnats Pass, they were ambushed by the miners who pulled them from their horses, struggling and screaming for help, and took all of the money they were carrying, £200. They then dragged them to a barn where they murdered them. Allan's throat was cut

Descent into Castleton through Winnats Pass.

Descent through Winnats Pass.

Early sketch of Winnats Pass.

from ear to ear and Clara was killed by a miner's pickaxe being driven into her head. Their bodies were then buried in a cave and not discovered for another ten years. Some days after the murders had been committed their horses were found at Sparrowpit and taken to Chatsworth; they were never claimed.

Although all of the miners escaped any form of British justice, they were nevertheless punished by divine justice. One of the miners, James Ashton, named the other men in the group in a deathbed confession some twenty years later, and testified that all had suffered in different ways. He himself had bought a number of horses with his share of the money, but the horses went lame. He had fallen into debt and lived the remainder of his life in isolation and penury. One of his accomplices, Thomas Hall, being filled with remorse for his actions, had hanged himself; Nicholas Cook had broken his neck at the Winnats near to the place where they had committed the murders, whilst Francis Butler had gone mad. The fifth felon, John Bradshaw, had been crushed by falling stone.

Many still hold to the belief that the ghosts of Allan and Clara, the ill-fated lovers, can still be seen wandering near to Winnats Pass, hand in hand.

Location: S33 8WA

The Story of Dorothy Vernon

When Elizabeth was Queen of England, Sir George Vernon was King of the Peak and Haddon Hall was his palace. Sir George's first wife was dead, leaving him with two daughters, Margaret and Dorothy. Margaret, the elder, was about to be married to a son of the Earl of Derby.

Sir George doted upon Dorothy, but it was Margaret who was the favourite of his second wife, Dame Maude, the scheming stepmother. She insisted that Dorothy sleep in her old nursery and perform menial tasks such as embroidery and tapestry. Luce, her childhood nurse, was her only companion.

Dorothy took early morning rambles in the wooded walks around Haddon Hall with Luce, where she met her lover, John Manners. On his daily visits, John was never recognised as he always appeared in disguise. As Dorothy's relationship blossomed, it came to the notice of Dame Maude, who ensured that Sir George also objected to the relationship. Sir George was reminded that after her marriage Margaret would become a countess and Dorothy should not be shackled with a mere soldier of fortune. Meanwhile, John Manners was busy enlisting the help of Will Dawson, the head forester of Haddon, who agreed to employ him as a woodman, and dressed him in a disguise. But, when Ben Shaw, a park-keeper on the estate, thought that Manners had designs on his lover, a pretty serving-maiden, he decided to watch Manners like a hawk. His first move was to conceal himself in the branches of an oak tree, but after witnessing a meeting between Manners and Dorothy and realising its significance, he went to Manners and said that he would act as a messenger between the lovers, as Luce, Dorothy's nurse, also happened to be his grandmother.

As Margaret was soon to be married to Sir Thomas Stanley, Sir George promised Dorothy's hand to his younger brother. As soon as the engagement

Dorothy Vernon's Door.

Haddon Hall (North view) in 1812.

became known, Manners urged Dorothy to elope with him. But, much as she wanted to agree with his plans, Dorothy felt that leaving her father without his consent would bring disgrace upon the family. John said that she must make up her mind. He pleaded with her and said that either she promised to elope with him on the night of her sister's wedding, or she would never see him again. Eventually, Dorothy agreed to his entreaty.

On the night of Margaret's marriage when all of the bridal rites had been conducted, the time had come for hours of unlimited festivity. There was an abundance of fish, flesh and fowl and the long oaken board groaned under the weight of boars' heads, barons of beef and haunches of venison. Whilst there was more than an ample sufficiency to eat, there was also a plentiful supply of alcohol. Then, when the revelry was at its height, Dorothy quietly excused herself and departed the scene. She went to her old nursery where Luce was waiting, carrying a thick cloak to throw over her ball-dress. It was almost midnight when Luce bade goodbye to Dorothy, watching her pass the pleasaunce, cross the river bridge and then fall into the waiting arms of John Manners. The lovers' route took them through Matlock Valley and then on along the Wye. They rested when they arrived at Allestree, on the outskirts of Derby. After procuring fresh horses and a more suitable riding habit for Dorothy, they passed through Derby on their way south, reaching Aylstone later that evening. They were married the following day.

A few days later a messenger arrived at Haddon carrying a letter from Dorothy and John. Sir George readily forgave his favourite daughter for her elopement, and it was only a short time before the couple were being welcomed back to the Peak.

Location: DE45 1LA

A Dream of Heaven

There once lived a young girl called Ann Brown in the small town of Eckington. One fateful day she fell into a trance and became very ill, so much so that her mother believed she was dead. After being left quietly in her bedroom for many hours, her mother ventured to go in and kiss goodbye to her much-loved daughter, but, much to her surprise, she thought that she could feel her daughter's breath warm upon her cheek. Finding herself in a state of shock, relief and jubilation, she immediately ran to the rectory and begged the parson to visit her. Upon his arrival the rector took a small mirror and held it to the young girl's mouth in order to see whether it became steamed by her breath. When the clergyman observed the mirror becoming clouded he immediately summoned the whole family into the girl's bed chamber and ordered them to stand around the bed. The rector himself stood at the head of the bed and took the maiden's hand into his own. After a little while the girl stirred, opened her eyes and uttered an involuntary sigh of relief. Then, addressing Ann directly, the clergyman said to her, Now tell us where you have been.

When Ann appeared to have regained all of her faculties, she spoke directly to the parson, but everyone around the bed could hear what she was saying. She related an incredible story about being taken all the way to Heaven where the first to meet her was the Devil himself. She said that he was holding a black book

Lane leading from Eckington
Parish Church.

Parish Church of St Peter and St Paul, Eckington.

in his hands, and the title on the book's cover was written in crimson. She said she had then been asked by the Devil to write her name in the book and follow him, but she had refused, saying, 'Get thee hence, Satan.' She had then continued on her way. Next, she recalled having seen an angel dressed in pure white, who took her hand and led her along a path as white as snow, which led to the gates of Heaven. She remembered that above the gates there was an inscription, which simply stated, 'Behold the Lamb'. Then, as she approached, the gates flew open and the Lord Jesus came out and took her in. She was taken to a place in which there were many girls just like herself. Continuing, she was then led to a place where there were many soldiers who were carrying spears and bayonets. Finally, another angel appeared and led her to a place that was full of infants singing. It was here that she saw the throne of God, but said that she had not been able to see God himself. She was then told by the Lord that it was God's wish that she should go back to the earth for a little while longer, but, even though she had pleaded to stay, the Lord had said that she should return to the world.

The rector and the family around the bed just stared in wonder and amazement after hearing of Ann's experience.

Location: S21 4EP

Tideswell's Markets and Singers

Tideswell is a very small and ancient town that lies approximately 5 miles west of Eyam. In 1251 Paulinus de Brampton was granted a charter to hold a weekly market in Tideswell every Wednesday. The charter also granted that a fair could be held between 23 June and 25 June, the festival of the decollation of St John the Baptist. However, it was not until 1393 that the weekly market was confirmed, and the dates of the annual fair changed to 28 August and 29 August. With a flourishing economy and population, the weekly markets continued to grow throughout the post-medieval period, and by the latter half of the eighteenth century there were three fairs being held annually: 3 May for cattle; the first Wednesday in September for sheep and cattle; and 18 October, also for sheep and cattle.

By 1846 the number of fairs had increased to five, with the last two being particularly important for the sale of cheese, in addition to cattle and sheep. Following the Enclosure Act of 1822, parcels of land at the northern end of the town were allocated to be used specifically for the annual fairs: a 2-acre plot at Town Head for sheep and a 4-acre site at Wheston Bank for cattle fairs. The land was held under a very strange tenure; the precentor of Lichfield, after a first payment of fifteen marks, should render yearly to Sir Richard Daniel, of Tideswell, or his heirs, one pair of white gloves at Easter and sixpence at Michaelmas. However, in former times, the vicar, in addition to being required to preach, was also held responsible for keeping a lamp burning in the church.

Church Lane,
Tideswell.

Above: Church of St John the Baptist, Tideswell, *c.* 1906.

Below: Church of St John the Baptist, Tideswell.

George Hotel, Tideswell.

Over the years Tideswell has produced many fine vocalists, none more famous than Samuel Slack. His undoubted talent was first noticed by Georgina, Duchess of Devonshire. She immediately sent him for training under Spofforth, the great master of singing. Although Slack was a somewhat ungainly and uncouth character, who liked, rather more than he should have done, both his pipe and his drink, there was no doubting his angelic voice.

On one occasion he was asked to sing for George III, and it appears that the king was very impressed. Slack's response was, 'Oh, he wer pleased, wor he? Ah, I know'd – I know'd I could dow't.'

On another occasion, when attending a provincial festival, Slack reverted to his usual habit by not associating with any of his fellow performers. Instead, he took himself off and imbibed on his own. When he'd had enough to drink he staggered into a field, lay down and slept until sobriety returned. In the morning, just as he was waking, a massive bull wandered over. Seeing the bull and being aware of the imminent danger, Slack gave a loud, deep-throated bellow. The bull, forgetting his own inherent ferocity, turned tail and ran off!

Location: SK17 8NU

Shrovetide Football

In 1683 Charles Cotton wrote about a game played in Ashbourne known as Shrovetide Football, although it is known that the game was being played for many years before that time. The game, which is ostensibly called football, is played over two days, on Shrove Tuesday and Ash Wednesday, and can include anything up to 10,000 players divided into two teams. The game amounts to little more than a moving brawl, and carries on over the town's streets, through nearby fields, and has even been known to continue into the river itself! Since the game was first played, very little, including two world wars, has interrupted the staging of the game. There was no game in either 1968 or 2002 because of the outbreak of foot-and-mouth disease.

In 1928 the game took a new title, the Royal Shrovetide Football game, when the then Prince of Wales, later to become Edward VIII, attended and 'turned up' the ball. The game was once again graced with a royal presence in 2003, when the current Prince of Wales, HRH Prince Charles, started the game by throwing the ball into play from a raised plinth. Tradition demands that the dignitary of the day is raised aloft near to Compton Bridge and then accompanied to a special lunch.

Above left: Ball used in 1977 jubilee game.

Above right: Down'ards Goal.

The opposing teams are traditionally known as Up'Ards and Down'Ards, simply meaning upwards and downwards, Up'Ards being players born north of Henmore Brook and Down'Ards players born south of the river. After the 'turn-up', which marks the start of the game, each team attempts to carry the ball back to their own goal, rather than attempting to score in the opponent's goal. The Up'Ards attempt to score at Sturston Mill, whereas the Down'Ards aim is to score in their goal at Clifton Mill, some 3 miles distant from the Up'Ards' goal. In order to 'goal' a ball, the players must actually be in the river!

The ball itself is larger than a standard football; it is painted and filled with cork so that it floats when thrown into the river. However, some townspeople believe that, originally, the 'ball' was a severed head that had been thrown into the crowd after a local execution.

The rules of the game are relatively simple: unnecessary violence is frowned upon and it is absolutely forbidden to commit murder or manslaughter during the game. Similarly, there are certain areas of the town that are out of bounds, and also, the ball must not be hidden at any time during the game. To score a goal the ball must be tapped three times in the area of the goal.

On both days the game starts at two o'clock and ends at ten o'clock in the evening. If the ball is 'goaled' before five-thirty in the afternoon, the game restarts. It remains the tradition that when the ball is 'goaled' the scorer is carried on the shoulders of his teammates to The Greenman Royal Hotel, where celebrations often continue for quite some time!

Location: DE6 1GT

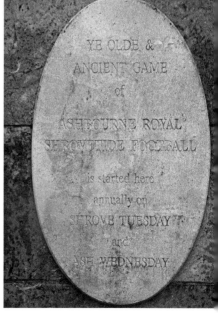

Above: The Greenman Royal Hotel.

Right: Plaque marking traditional starting point of Shrovetide Football game.

Castleton Church

The building of the perimeter wall for Peveril Castle began in 1086, and the village of Castleton itself sprang up at the base of the hill. William Peveril, the illegitimate son of William the Conqueror, built the church sometime towards the end of the eleventh century, which, for many years, was known as the Church of Peak Castle. Initially, the church was not built as a church but as a garrison chapel for soldiers stationed in the castle. In later years the church was called St Edmund's, a name it still retains.

From time immemorial, the ancient church at Castleton has always celebrated the festival known as Restoration Day. The festival, which is observed on 29 May, is more commonly known as Oak Apple Day or Royal Oak Day, and commemorates the restoration of the English monarchy in May 1660.

The day's festivities begin with a parade through the town, headed by a man on horseback who carries a large decorated garland. The celebrations continue throughout the day then, in the early evening, the garland is carried to the church tower where it is raised to the summit by an elaborate pulley mechanism. The garland is then carefully located on the central pinnacle on the south side, the other pinnacles having been adorned with oak boughs at an early hour in the morning.

Above: Early morning scene along Cross Street, Castleton.

Left: Interior of St Edmund's Church, Castleton.

> The parable of the vinegar. **S.**
>
> chief priests and the scribes came upon hir
> with the elders,
>
> 2 And spake unto him, saying, Tell u
> By what authority doest thou these things
> or who is he that gave thee this authority?
>
> 3 And he answered and said unto them

Above: Parable of the Vinegar.

Right: St Edmund's Parish Church, Castleton.

The garlands remain there until the following year's celebrations. Reference to the parish register shows that the festival of Restoration Day has long been a feature of parish life in Castleton, as an entry dated 1749 declares: 'paid for an iron rod to hang ye ringer's garland in, 8d.'

A particularly interesting feature of St Edmund's Church itself is the library of rare books, which is housed in the church's vestry. The collection was donated to the parish by a former vicar, and are 'to be lent out to the parishioners at the discretion of the minister'. The small library contains such works as Newcome's *History of the Abbey of St Alban*, which was printed in 1793. There are also two early copies of the English version of the Bible, one of these being 'Cranmer's Bible', issued in 1539. The other, bearing the date 1611, is a so-called 'Breeches Bible'. In more recent editions of the Bible, chap. iii. verse 7 in the Book of Genesis states, 'And they sewed fig leaves together, and made themselves aprons,' whereas in the Castleton Bible the translation is, 'They sewed figge leaves together and made themselves breeches.' Apparently, it was considered that 'breeches' sounded a little too vulgar. Another unique book in the church's collection is the bible known as The Vinegar Bible. Because of typographical errors, the Parable of the Vineyard was printed as The Parable of the Vinegar.

Location: S33 8WE

The Murder of Dr Cuddie

Formerly a navy surgeon, Dr William Cuddie moved to the tiny village of Winster to continue practising his profession, and it was in this capacity that he first met Miss Mary Brittlebank, the daughter of an eminent solicitor. As Mary was in a delicate state of health, Cuddie was required to make regular visits to the Brittlebank residence. A strong romantic relationship developed between the doctor and his patient, much to the annoyance of her family. One afternoon whilst walking together they were accosted by one of her brothers, Mr William Brittlebank. After some sharp words had been exchanged, William Brittlebank took his sister away.

However, William Brittlebank took exception to the language that the doctor had used and promptly had a message sent to him, challenging him to a duel that very evening. Dr Cuddie did not respond, so another message was sent to him on the following morning. Dr Cuddie informed the messenger that he would not meet with Mr William Brittlebank. Needless to say, Mr Brittlebank was not pleased with this response. He asked a mutual friend, Mr Spencer, a surgeon who lived in Bakewell, to accompany him and his brother, Mr Francis Brittlebank, to Dr Cuddie's house. When they arrived at the house they were joined by a third brother, Mr Andrew Brittlebank. Mr Spencer then went into the house where he informed Dr Cuddie that he must either make some sort of apology to

Bank House, the home of Dr Cuddie.

Winster Hall.

Mr William Brittlebank or fight. Initially the doctor declined to do either, but, after some cajoling by Mr Spencer, he appears to have consented. Pistols were supplied and, walking out into Dr Cuddie's garden, the men faced each other. When the signal to fire was given, Cuddie received a wound to his abdomen. He died the following day.

All three brothers together with Mr Spencer were tried on a charge of wilful murder. The trial of the parties was held at the Derby Assizes before Mr Justice Park. The murder itself was charged to have been committed by Mr William Brittlebank, and the other prisoners stood trial for aiding, abetting and assisting in said murder. Mr William Brittlebank absconded, but the other three were conveyed to Derby jail.

During the trial, background details were given relating to both Dr Cuddie and the Brittlebank family, and then the court was taken through the events that, ultimately, led to the death of Dr Cuddie.

It was alleged that on 21 May a letter was sent to the doctor in which he, Brittlebank, complained about the insult he said he had received, and challenged the doctor to either apologise for the insult or to fight him in order to expiate that insult. Mr Cuddie refused to honour the letter with any answer.

On the following day Spencer arrived and agreed to take a note to the doctor asking for either an apology or, failing that, challenging him to a fight. Cuddie's reply indicated that he believed that he didn't have any apology to make, nor would he meet Mr Brittlebank in a duel. After further negotiation, Cuddie agreed

Above: Winster Wesleyan Chapel.

Left: Winster Market House.

to talk to Mr Brittlebank in the garden. However, when Cuddie ventured into his garden he encountered the three Brittlebank brothers. Andrew Brittlebank, anxious to prevent the duel, implored the doctor to apologise. Then, when Cuddie declined to do so, pistols were produced and the protagonists stood some 15 yards apart before firing.

Sometime after the duel, when Cuddie was lying on his deathbed, he made the following declaration:

> The declaration of William Cuddie, of Winster, surgeon, made before me, Philip Gell, Esq., one of his Majesty's justices of the peace for the county of Derby, this 22nd day of May, 1821, who saith, that he was called upon by William Brittlebank, of Winster, to fight a duel, and that he wished to avoid doing so. That Edmund Spencer, of Bakewell, surgeon, came to him on the 22nd of May, instant, and told him that William Brittlebank and his brothers were in the garden waiting for him, and that he, William Cuddie, must make an apology, or fight. That he, William Cuddie, went to the garden, and refused to make an apology. That Edmund Spencer opened his coat and showed him two pistols, one of which he took, and William Brittlebank took the other; that they separated to the distance of fifteen yards, or more. That Edmund Spencer threw up his hat as a signal and they both fired their pistols as near together as possible.

After an absence of an hour and twenty minutes the jury returned a verdict of 'not guilty' in favour of the prisoners.

Location: DE4 2DQ (Bank House, Dr Cuddie's home and scene of the duel.)

Bakewell Tart

The market town of Bakewell in the Derbyshire Dales is synonymous with the Bakewell pudding. Although shrouded in mystery as to the true origin of this famous delicacy, there seems to be widespread agreement that the 'pudding' was first created by accident. Mrs Greaves, the landlady of the White Horse coaching inn in the town, was expecting some special guests for supper that evening. During the meticulous preparations that were being made for the dinner, she was called away on important business, leaving the final preparations to her inexperienced cook, Mrs Wilson, the wife of a local candle maker and chandler. Clear instructions were given as to the preparation of the inn's most popular sweet, strawberry jam tarts, but Mrs Wilson apparently became confused when looking at the array of ingredients she saw laid out in front of her. The pudding should have been made with an egg mixture, an almond paste pastry base and a topping of strawberry jam, but instead of mixing the eggs and almond paste into the pastry, Mrs Wilson had put the

Bridge Street, Bakewell.

Above: Packhorse bridge over the River Wye, Bakewell.

Below: Rutland Arms Hotel.

The Old Original
Bakewell
Pudding Shop.

jam into the base first and then spread the mixture over the top. When the dish was taken from the oven, the egg and almond paste had set like an egg custard, but the guests at the inn were so pleased with the sweet that Mrs Greaves made sure that the dish continued to be prepared in exactly the same way. So, rather than being seen as a complete disaster, the 'pudding' was hailed as being a culinary triumph and soon became the most popular dish at the inn. Meanwhile, Mrs Wilson immediately saw the possibility of making the puddings as a commercial venture. She bought the recipe and set up in business in the cottage where her husband also made candles. The cottage where they lived and had their manufactory is now known as the Old Original Bakewell Pudding Shop and is still serving Bakewell puddings, made from the original recipe. Another bakery, Bloomer's, which is to be found just around the corner from the Old Original Bakewell Pudding Shop, also claims to sell Bakewell puddings using the 'first and only genuine recipe handed down over four generations'. The only definitive statement that can be made regarding these counter-claims is that both bakeries make extremely fine Bakewell puddings.

The recipe for Bakewell pudding soon began to appear in cookery books and magazines; one of the earliest journals to feature the recipe was *The Magazine of Domestic Economy*, which was issued in London in 1836, and afterwards, in 1861, Mrs Beeton published a recipe for Bakewell pudding in *The Book of Household Management*.

Location: DE45 1BT

The Man Who Stole the Parson's Sheep

There was once a poor man who lived with his family in Calver, and every year at Christmastide he stole a fat sheep so that he could give his family a few special dinners during the festive period. One Christmas, quite by accident, he happened to steal one of the sheep belonging to the vicar of the local church at Curbar, Parson Brown. The following day, one of the man's sons, a young boy of around twelve years of age, could be heard singing the following verse around the village:

> My father's stolen the parson's sheep,
> And a merry Christmas we shall keep,
> We shall have both pudding and meat,
> But you moant say nought about it.

A few days later, as the parson was walking around the village on his parochial duties, he happened to hear the young boy singing his ditty. He walked over to the lad and complemented him on his singing. Furthermore, he asked him if he'd come over to the church on Sunday evening and sing his song in church. Feeling highly honoured that the rector thought so much of his singing, he readily agreed to the request, but then remembered that he didn't own any clothes which were suitable to go to church in. As soon as the rector heard this, he promised to buy some clothes for him, providing that he sang in front of the congregation. On Sunday evening the young lad turned up for church dressed in his new clothes and when the service was over, the parson got to his feet and said, 'Stay, my brethren, I want you to hear what this boy has to sing, it's gospel truth that he'll tell you.'

The parson was obviously hoping that the boy's verse would incriminate his father, but when he stood up, the boy's song was very different from what the parson had been expecting.

> As I was in the field one day
> I saw the parson kiss a may*
> He gave me a shilling not to tell,
> And these new clothes do fit me well.

*maid

Above: River Derwent at Curbar.

Below: The Bridge Inn, Calver Bridge.

The Parish Church of All Saints, Curbar.

Upon hearing the boy's ditty, the parson jumped to his feet and said that it was a pack of lies, but the folks in the church didn't believe him. They ran out and declared that the parson was a fraud. He was never seen in the church or the village again.

Location: S32 3YU

The Legend of Swarkestone Bridge

Swarkestone Bridge, first mentioned in 1204, was originally known as the 'Ponte de Cordy' and was built to cross the River Trent and the surrounding marshes. Although the Trent is no wider than 414 feet at this point, the bridge itself is 1,304 yards long and has a total of seventeen arches along its length. It is thought that the Trent was first spanned at Swarkestone in order to accommodate the advance of King John's army to the north; this occurred towards the end of 1215. As a temporary structure the bridge would, in all probability, have been a wooden construction, and built of stone only after reconstruction. In all events, records show that a bridge had been established here long before the accession of Edward I in November 1272. The bridge is still the longest stone-built bridge in England.

There are many local legends relating to the bridge; the most popular one relates to the two Bellamont sisters. The sisters were the daughters of the local lord of the manor, and both had become betrothed to two knights in the shire. After the engagements had been formally announced their father organised

Above: Early photograph of Swarkestone Bridge.

Right: Approach to Swarkestone Causeway.

a grand feast at Swarkestone Hall, which included tilting, hunting, hawking, and other medieval sports, but the festivities were abruptly halted by an urgent message requiring the lord of the manor and the knights to join forthwith an assembly of barons who were engaged in hot dispute with the tyrannical king. Horses were readied, and they set off across the Trent to meet with the barons. The call of national duty was promptly answered.

At the conclusion of their meeting the knights were anxious to return to their betrothed, leaving the earl with his esquires and pages to return at a more leisurely pace. Unfortunately, there had been a downpour during their time with the barons, and the river had risen to a dangerously high level. Undeterred, the two knights spurred their tired horses on. They crossed the meadows safely, but, as darkness was now falling, they either missed the ford or were swept off it by the raging torrent. Both were drowned within sight of the lighted windows of the hall.

When news reached the manor where the celebrations were still in full swing, the sisters were devastated, and considered themselves to be widows and, in keeping with the prevailing spirit of the times, devoted the rest of their lives to the memory of their deceased lovers. In order to commemorate the tragic accident, they vowed to build a bridge across the river so that a similar fate would not befall travellers in the future. The bridge was commissioned, but due to the high construction and maintenance costs, both sisters died in poverty having exhausted their collective fortunes. Neither sister married, never having been able to come to terms with the tragedy that had befallen them. Many people are still of the belief that the bridge is haunted by the ghosts of the two sisters.

Location: DE73 7GW

River Trent at Swarkestone.

Above: Sketch of Swarkestone Bridge.

Below: Swarkestone Bridge.

Some Old Burial Customs in Derbyshire

Whenever a funeral was held at Castleton, burying cakes and warm ale were handed round. There is some disagreement as to the shape and size of the burying cakes. Some folk believe that the cake must be three-cornered, and, for some reason, big enough to be carried under the arm. Others are of the opinion that burying cakes must be round and have a diameter of 7 or 8 inches. But, whatever the shape and size, burying cakes were cut into slices before being handed around to the mourners, together with a measure of warm ale.

It was also the tradition in the village that, if the person being buried was particularly impoverished, then mourners would have a collection to help towards the funeral expenses. These funerals, which were common, were known as 'pay-buryings'. Contributions were collected by an old woman who sat in an armchair near to the fire, or, if it was a particularly warm day, she sat in a quiet corner on an upright chair.

In the nearby village of Bradwell, an old farmer, Jacob Eyre, was required to attend all funerals. During the funeral a basket, like a butter basket, hung on one of Eyre's arms, and with the other arm he dispensed pieces of bread to village children who stood outside around the door. In fact, the children loitered there just to receive the bread. The bread that Eyre gave out was no bigger than 3 or 4 inches square and was obtained from the bakehouse or relatives of the deceased provided it themselves. Eyre was a great favourite with the village children, but the custom of giving out pieces of bread stopped more or less straight after he died.

At Abney, near to Eyam, Mrs Middleton's mother used to dress coffins with flowers, but she never put thyme on them, believing that 'they had nothing to do with time'. But at Bradwell, whenever one of the Twelve Oddfellows died, the surviving Oddfellows marched before his coffin, singing and carrying a sprig of thyme. The thyme was then thrown on top of the coffin as the Oddfellow was interred. Thyme was also placed around the house of the deceased immediately after the death, and remained there until the funeral. In and around Abney, Thyme was often known as 'southern wood', 'old man', or 'lad's love'.

Location: Throughout Derbyshire

Dicky of Tunsted

The tiny village of Tunsted (Tunstead) lies midway between Chapel-en-le-Frith and Whaley. At one time the house occupied by Mr Samuel Dickson housed 'the mysterious skull'. It was always considered that the skull was female, but that prompts the question as to why it was baptized with a masculine name. Dicky's exploits were well known in the area, but the story is more mysterious than it appears to be on the surface. Apparently, there were two co-heiresses living at the property, but, rather unfortunately, they were both in love with the same man. Totally frustrated with the situation, one sister decided that the best way to end the rivalry was to murder her sister. Then, in her dying moments it was recorded that she made a threat to the effect that unless her bones remained in the house forever, then she would create mayhem for anyone who lived there. Her skull was duly retained in the house to comply with her wishes. Many 'doings' were subsequently attributed to the skull, and the apparition that accompanied it. Mr J. Bramwell, a former owner of the property, declared that the apparition of the skull prevented the house and farm from being robbed, and that it was worth more to him than his best cow. Another neighbour, Mr A. Fox, told the story of the time when the skull was buried in Chapel-en-le-Frith churchyard, but the apparition appeared, and then commenced 'weeping and wailing', if not 'gnashing of teeth'; cattle strayed, some died, others came to sundry misfortunes, and during the 'witching hours of night' furniture in many of the farms and the church was turned upside down in utter confusion. In desperation, it was suggested to the then occupant of the farm that it might be advisable to exhume the skull and restore it to its old quarters – an old cheese vat at the bottom of the staircase. As soon as the exhumation had been completed, order was restored. In later years the house underwent significant restoration and, by way of oversight, Dicky was thrown away. But then, as had happened previously, the spectre appeared. The workmen ran, terrified as to what they were witnessing. Furthermore, when they did recommence their labours, they found that their previous day's work had been damaged overnight. They also reported that whilst they were hammering and hewing, they could occasionally hear a low unearthly moan. In desperation they searched for the skull and replaced it as before; after being restored to its former resting place all was well. But there were many positive aspects of Dicky's 'doings': if a cow was near to calving in the night, Dicky or the ghost would give an alarm; or, if there was an approaching death of a relative or friend, Dicky could always be relied upon to issue some sort of warning.

Above: Entrance to the village of Tunstead Milton.

Below: Hills around Tunstead Milton.

The tranquil water of Combs Reservoir.

Before leaving the neighbourhood of Chapel-en-le-Frith, it is worth glancing at a particularly noteworthy entry in the town's register for 1716:

On March the 16th, 1716, one Poenix, a girl about 13 years of age, a parish apprentice with W. Ward, of Peak Forest, went from George Bowden's house, at Lane-end, about five o'clock in the morning towards her master's house. She sat down on Peaslow, between the ruts on G. Bowden's road, and stayed that day and the next, and the Friday, Saturday, and Sunday following, two of which days – viz, the 16th and 17th – were the most severe for snowing and driving that hath been seen in the memory of man. She was found alive on Monday, about one o'clock, by W. Jackson, of Sparrow Pit, and W. Longden, of Peak Forest, and after a slender refreshment of a little hot milk, was carried in her master's house, and is now (March 25th, 1717), very well, only a little stiffness in her limbs. This was the Lord's doing, and will be marvellous in future generations. She eat [sic] no meat during the six days, nor was she hungry, but very thirsty, and slept much.

Location: SK23 7ES

The Girl Who Got Up the Tree

After serving for an agreed length of time on a farm near to Edale in the northern part of the county, a young girl was due to return home to her family. Before she departed she told her sweetheart that she would meet him near to a stile where they had met many times before. The stile itself was overhung by a gnarled oak tree. After she'd finished her work for the day the girl made her way to the stile. She got there before her sweetheart, only to find that somebody had dug a hole underneath the tree, and lying by the side of the hole she noticed that there was a pickaxe and a spade. This discovery made her feel very uneasy, so, for her own safety, she decided to climb up into the tree and hide there until her sweetheart arrived. A few minutes later her sweetheart did arrive, but he had another man with him. It was obvious that they thought she had not arrived as they started talking. Her sweetheart said, 'She will not come to-night. We'll go home now, and come back and kill her to-morrow night.' When she was sure that the two men

Entrance to the village of Edale.

Above: Grinds Brook, Edale.

Below: The Church of the Holy and Undivided Trinity, Edale.

had gone, the girl came down the tree and ran home to her father. She told him exactly what she'd seen and heard at the stile. As soon as he'd given the matter some thought, he outlined his plans to his daughter: 'We will have a feast and ask our friends, and we will ask thy sweetheart to come and the man that came with him to the tree.'

The feast went ahead and the two men came along, together with the other guests. In the evening many in the group started to ask riddles of each other. Eventually, when everyone else had given their riddles, the girl who had climbed up the tree decided that it was time to ask hers. With all of the party gathered around, she delivered her riddle:

> One moonlight night as I sat high
> Waiting for one but two came by,
> The boughs did bend, my heart did quake
> To see the hole the fox did make.

When the two men heard the girl's riddle they quickly departed and were never seen again.

Location: S33 7ZA

Well Dressing

The custom of 'well dressing' must be one of the most famous, if not *the* most famous, traditions still observed throughout Derbyshire. The custom was originally thought to have been a pagan rite held in honour of the nymphs, and corresponded with the ancient Roman Fontinalia, or annual flower festival of the spirits of the streams and fountains. The practice has since been adapted to Christian usage. Derbyshire is now widely acknowledged to be the home of well dressing.

At Tissington the celebration occurs on Ascension Day, and one writer was moved to observe that 'Tissington's well-dressing is a festivity which is heartily loved and earnestly anticipated, one which draws the hearts of those who were brought up there, but whom fortune has cast in distant places, homeward with an irresistible charm.' Elaborate preparations are made for its approach.

At Derby and Wirksworth the celebration is held at Whitsuntide, whereas at Goulgrave the custom is observed on 24 June, Midsummer Day.

Traditionally, flowers are arranged in patterns to form mottos and texts from scripture, or crosses and crowns, with greenery to complete the picture.

Above left: An early sketch of St Anne's Well, Buxton.

Above right: Bowden Lane Well, 2019.

The well itself is adorned with a large wooden framework erected in front of it, and covered with a base layer of clay. On occasions, the structure upon which the tableau is arranged can be as high as 12 feet, with the wooden erection being in the form of an arch or some other suitable design. The next stage in the erection of the structure is to lay plaster of Paris over the wooden structure and, whilst still wet, flowers without leaves are pressed in, forming a series of beautiful mosaic patterns. Large yellow field ranunculus are often used in these arrangements, as are violets and daisies. Other flowers, such as coral berries from holly, mountain ash, and yew, are also gathered and carefully stored in winter to be ready for the May Day fete. Garnishing the summit of the edifice is the text 'O ye wells, bless ye the Lord!' Finally, the pure sparkling water, which pours down from the midst of them onto the rustic moss-grown stones beneath, completes the picture and continues to make well dressing one of the most popular of all English customs.

Chapel-en-le-Frith Well Dressing, 2019.

Above left: Foolow Well Dressing, 2011.

Above right: Town Well, Chapel-en-le-Frith, 2019.

Folks gather around the first well while the ever-present clergyman reads the first of the three psalms appointed for the day. It is then traditional for a hymn, such as 'Rock of Ages' or 'A Living Stream so Crystal Clear' to be sung. Following this, the assembled group move to the next well where another psalm is read and another hymn is sung. When the party reaches the last two wells the Epistle and Gospel for the day are read. This ritual is attributed, by many, to the time in 1615 when a great drought visited Derbyshire, but the wells of Tissington continued to flow and provided enough water for the whole neighbourhood. Other scholars still maintain however that the custom dates back to Roman times, and connect it with an ancient pagan festival.

When the ceremony comes to an end, the afternoon is filled with the crowning of the May Queen and maypole dancing. In the evening the band plays for general dancing, and many of the maypole dances are repeated. The holiday atmosphere of the day is brought to an end with a display of fireworks.

Location: DE6 1RA

The Brutal Murder of Harriet Wager

An horrendous crime was reported in the *Sheffield Independent* and sometime later in *The Mercury* in Hobart, Australia. The events on the day in question are as follows:

On Christmas Eve 1866, the body of a married woman, Harriet Wager, was found in Vein dam, near her husband's house. The unfortunate deceased was the wife of a farmer named Edward Wager, who resided at Bleaklow Farm, near Calver. Wager had quite a reputation in the town, having spent some time in prison on account of his violent nature. Harriet Wager's marriage seems to have been blighted from the outset, as Wager had assaulted her on their wedding day.

Some days later, a friend of Harriet's, Alice Hancock from Sheffield, who was spending Christmas in the neighbourhood, called to see her. She was about to take her leave when Wager attempted to kiss her or to take some other liberty with her. Totally dumfounded and outraged, the young woman screamed and ran away. Harriet went out to see what was going on, and very soon assessed the situation. She told him, in no uncertain terms, that if anything like this ever happened again, she would have no hesitation in leaving him. Wager immediately returned to the house and proceeded to assault his wife. Later on two men, who happened to be working in the neighbourhood, were startled by some loud piercing shrieks. When they approached Wager's house, they saw Harriet running away from her husband, and were horrified by seeing that the whole of the lower part of her face was covered with blood. Seeing them, Harriet cried out for their assistance, but they were too afraid to interfere and walked on. They then saw Harriet fall to her knees, as if imploring her husband for mercy. At this time she was on the bank of the Vein dam. Then the two men, realising that something calamitous was about to happen, headed off to the village to seek assistance. As they looked back, they saw the unfortunate Harriet in the act of falling from the bank into the dam. It was difficult to tell whether the poor woman had been pushed by her husband or whether she overbalanced and accidently fell. Although the water was fairly shallow at this point, Wager didn't jump in to rescue her, but called over the men to assist him. They refused, so Wager did no more than return to his home. The two men went straight to Inspector Cruit. When he arrived shortly afterwards, he found the battered and bruised body of Mrs Wager in the water.

Above left: Calver Village today.

Above right: Countryside around Bleaklow Farm.

When Inspector Cruit went to Wager's house he found him sitting in a chair, his head in his hands, and making a moaning noise. Wager was taken into custody and initially charged with being accessory to his wife's death. The medical evidence revealed at the inquest at Hassop showed that there were serious lacerations of the liver and other injuries, and that the woman would probably have died in a few days from her husband's violence if she had not been drowned. The prisoner himself made a statement which, in essence, corroborated the facts already known with some minor variations.

Edward Wager was found guilty of 'wilfully and of malice aforethought, killing and murdering Harriett Wager' at Derbyshire Assizes. However, the matter was raised in the House of Commons where Mr Walpole told parliament that the last punishment of the law should not be applied where a murder had not been premeditated. He recommended Queen Victoria to exercise the royal prerogative of granting a reprieve. Wager's death sentence was commuted to penal servitude for life.

Location: S32 3AB

A Bizarre Marriage

One winter's day in 1684 the rector of Eyam, Revd Joseph Hunt, had been called to the Miners Arms to perform the office of baptism, as the landlord's infant son had suddenly taken ill. Having baptised the child the landlord, Mr Matthew Fearns, invited the rector to stay and enjoy a drink or two with some of the village's miners who were sat in the bar enjoying a well-earned couple of pints at the end of a long week. The rector took the landlord at his word, and enjoyed his hospitality and the company of the miners until he became totally inebriated. Now, it was well known in the village, especially amongst the miners in the community, that the landlord had a very charming and beautiful daughter, Ann, who, at the tender age of eighteen, was destined to break many hearts. Before very long Revd Hunt was seen entering into flirtatious conversation with the

Church Street, Eyam.

Miners Arms, Eyam.

young woman. As is often the case when large quantities of ale are consumed, one thing led to another and, 'egged on' by the miners, the rector, enjoying the prevailing mood and one or two drinks too many, agreed to participate in a mock wedding with the publican's daughter. The miners had little trust in the rector's promise, so they insisted that he should honour his promise there and then. After imbibing in another glass or two, the rector consented to go ahead with the ceremony. Without further ado, one of the miners produced a Book of Common Prayer and promptly acted as officiant. He read through the whole of the solemn ceremony, with the young girl and the rector performing the roles of bride and groom, respectively.

News of the event quickly spread throughout the neighbourhood, and before very long the unfortunate act of theatre came to the notice of the Bishop of the Diocese. He had no hesitation in commanding the beleaguered rector to legitimise the mock wedding, declaring that he must fulfil in earnest what he had done in jest. Although Hunt was already engaged to another lady from Derby, he duly complied with this edict and legally married Miss Fearns (Furness) on 4 September 1684. This action had unfortunate consequences, as the lady from Derby, who was very wealthy, took out an action for breach of promise against him. Many of Hunt's subsequent years were occupied in legal proceedings. The legal expenses alone ensured that he lost what little money he had, but the stigma of his actions soon lost him his friends in the village, whilst the reality of his actions meant that he was continually harassed by the officers of the law.

The Parish
Church of
St Lawrence,
Eyam.

Desperate to escape from the multitude of pressures which were besetting him, Hunt, together with his new bride, took refuge in the vestry, which, supposedly, had been built for the specific purpose of providing him with a place of refuge from his enemies. He dwelt in the vestry, together with his wife and nine children, until his death. In later years he was characterised as being of a very friendly disposition, with young people from the parish visiting him in his abode, where they would sit round the fire telling tales to while away the dreary winter nights.

Revd Joseph Hunt was rector at Eyam between 1683 and 1709. He resided in his makeshift dwelling until his death. There is a tombstone in a corner of the churchyard which records his death and the death of his wife. It simply states that Revd Joseph Hunt, rector of Eyam, was buried on 16 December 1709 and Ann, his wife, was buried on 18 December 1703.

Location: S32 5RG

Dale Abbey and the Legend of the Derby Baker

At the beginning of the twelfth century there lived in the parish of St Mary's in the City of Derby a devout and God-fearing baker. Because of his undoubted love of his fellow neighbours he was often compared to the Biblical Roman centurion Cornelius, and he was sometimes known by that name. His love of God and his desire to serve Him and the townsfolk of Derby meant that every Sunday Cornelius was given to distributing surplus food and clothing to the poor and destitute. When Cornelius was having his midday sleep one day the Blessed Virgin Mary appeared to him and told him that his work and devotion was pleasing to God, and that he should leave his family and friends and go to a place known as Depedale. There he would serve God in hunger, thirst, coldness and nakedness. Cornelius had little or no knowledge of a place called Depedale, but he went forward in faith, leaving his family and all of his possessions in Derby. At length he reached the tiny village of Stanley where he heard a woman telling her daughter to lead their cattle to Depedale. He accompanied the young woman on her journey, but when he arrived, he found a barren, marshy wasteland. After searching for some time, he was fortunate to find an outcrop of soft sandstone where he could build his hermitage. Cornelius continued to worship and live in

Abbey Field.

All Saints' Church, Dale Abbey.

solitude until one day, when sheltering from the cold, the smoke from his fire was seen by Ralph Fitz-Geremund, Lord of the Manor of Ockbrook and Alvaston, who had travelled over from Normandy with his friends to hunt in his English woods. On seeing the fire, he rode over intent on driving the intruder off his land, but when he heard of the hermit's poverty and pious life he was filled with compassion and allowed him to remain, and also granted him the tithe money from Borrowash Mill. This small income enabled the hermit to build a small chapel and home.

When the hermit died his dwelling became a place of pilgrimage and religious significance.

Then, in 1162, Dale Abbey began its life when a group of Augustinian monks arrived from their former home at Calke Priory and moved onto a site close to the hermit's cave. Some twenty years later they were replaced by Premonstratensian Canons (known as White Canons in England) from Tupholme. A few years after this they were joined by another group of Premonstratensians from Welbeck. It is said that when the abbey was founded in 1204, the king granted to the prior as much land as he could encircle with a plough drawn by two deer, between sunrise and sunset, but before the abbey could be built, the monks had to clear most of the forest and drain the land surrounding their site at Depedale. It was many years before the land was suitable for growing crops, but the abbey did eventually become self-supporting due, in large measure, to the gift of the town of Stanley to the Premonstratensian order by Geofrey de Salicosa and his wife Matilda, which ensured a more secure future. The new abbey became known as the Church of St Mary of Stanley Park. Eventually, the abbey owned somewhere in the region of 24,000 acres of land, although most of this would have been leased or rented

Right: Remains of
St Mary's Abbey.

Below: The Carpenters
Arms, where many
years ago cockfights
were reputed to have
been held.

Village of Dale Abbey.

out to local farmers, and some would have been used for the production of food for the monks.

In addition to giving sanctuary to weary travellers and providing for the spiritual needs of local townsfolk, the monks also cared for the sick and provided a refuge for lepers – an oratory was built halfway between the abbey buildings and the hermitage. The building was later to become the parish church.

The Act of Dissolution was signed by Henry VIII on 24 October 1539, thus ending almost four centuries of monastic life in Dale Abbey. Today all that remains of the abbey is the arch of the east window and the remains of the gatehouse to the rear of the Gateway Centre.

Location: DE7 4PN

The Death of Ann Hoon

The parish church in Longford was the setting for the marriage of twenty-one-year-old Ann Rollstone to Thomas Hoon. Before the first anniversary of their marriage, they were blessed with the birth of a daughter whom they named Elizabeth. Sadly, baby Elizabeth died in April of the following year, but Ann and Thomas were soon to find happiness again when another daughter was born in January 1795. They were overjoyed at the birth and called the baby Ann.

Life in the Hoon household went on much as usual, with Thomas continuing his work as a labourer and Ann taking the role of housewife. However, their domestic happiness was short-lived. One Friday, when Ann was making preparations for the evening meal and finding herself short of wood to heat the oven, she took some palings from a neighbour's garden fence. When she was threatened with prosecution and possible deportation, her mind 'went into overdrive' and her life was never to be the same again. She conceived of a plan which would mean that

St Chad's Church, Longford.

she would never again be separated from baby Ann. She put her plan into action and then submitted herself to the magistrates. She was tried at Derby Assizes.

The tragic tale was reported in local newspapers and a detailed account was also given in the Annual Register for the year 1798:

> What particularly engaged the attention of the public at our assizes was a charge against a woman of the name of Ann Hoon aged 24 for the wilful murder of her infant child about 14 months old. The circumstances of this murder were as follows: On Friday last this poor creature who is the wife of a labouring man was about to heat her oven and being short of wood had broken down a rail or two from the fencing round the plantation of a gentleman in the neighbourhood some of her neighbours threatened her with a prosecution and told her she would be transported for it. This much alarmed her mind and the idea of being separated from her child of whom she had always appeared remarkably fond so wrought on her imagination that she formed the horrible design of putting it to death in order that by surrendering herself into the hands of justice she might be executed for the murder and so be forever reunited in heaven to that babe whom she had loved more than life. As soon therefore as her husband was gone out to his labour she proceeded to put this diabolical design into execution she filled a large tub with water when the babe smiling in its mother's face disarmed her for the moment and she found herself unable to commit the horrid act. She then lulled the babe to sleep at her breast and wrapping a cloth round it plunged it into the tub and held it under water till life became extinct then took it out of the tub and laid it on the bed and taking her hat and cloak locked her street door and left her key at a neighbour's for her husband when he should return from his labour. She then proceeded to walk eight or nine miles to a magistrate and requesting admission to him told him the whole story concluding with an earnest desire immediately to be executed. She was tried this morning and many strong instances of insanity for some years past appearing the Jury found her not guilty.

Location: DE6 3DS

The Bodies on the Moors

The village of Hope holds many mysteries, not least of which is a story that relates to the moors around the parish and a most extraordinary occurrence concerning the preservation of human bodies buried in them.

A grazier and his female servant set out one day in 1674 to cross the moors on their way to a new life in Ireland. They became lost in the heavy snow which, that year, covered the moors from January until May. Sometime later when their bodies were found, the coroner decreed that the corpses were so offensive and disfigured that they should be buried directly where they had been located. There was then a period of twenty-nine years when the ground where they lay wasn't touched. But, when the makeshift burial place was opened, it was found that there was no discernible change in the bodies; their skin was a normal colour,

Daggers House, Hope.

Moors behind the village of Hope.

being fair and natural, and their flesh was soft to the touch, as though they had only recently died. Apart from being exposed on a number of occasions as a spectacle, the bodies were carefully covered again and left buried for a further twenty years, laying some 3 feet deep in moist soil and moss.

In 1716, some forty-two years after the tragedy, it was deemed that a partial inspection of the bodies should be made. On that occasion the rector of Hope, Revd Jacob Creswell, was asked to be present to witness the inspection. When the stockings were drawn off the man's legs, although they had not been uncovered before, it was found that their condition was seen to be 'quite fair'. When the man's flesh was pressed with the fingers it pitted a little but remained firm. The joints were also found to have remained relatively supple and free from any stiffness. When examining their clothing, it was noted that the woman had been wearing a new serge garment which, to all intents and purposes, remained in the same condition as the day that she had died.

The mystery of the bodies on the moors has still not been explained.

Location: S33 6AA

Above: Parish Church of St Peter, Hope.

Below: Woodroffe Arms, Hope.

Alice Phoenix

The town of Chapel-en-le-Frith is characterised by the pleasant gritstone houses that sprang up around the ancient chapel of the forest. The original building was for many centuries frequented by the foresters and deer-keepers of the Peak, but fell into disrepair before a new church was built and dedicated to St Thomas à Becket. The church, as a centre of the local community, has over the centuries gathered many historic memories. In 1591 it was used as a Court of Justice, then, following the battle at Ribblesdale Moor in 1648 and the defeat of the Scottish army at Preston, the church was used as a prison for sixteen days holding some 1,500 prisoners.

Also written in the registers is the strange story of a young maiden named Alice Phoenix (Phenix), a parish apprentice who in 1717 was overtaken by a storm when on her way to her master's house at Peak Forest:

1717, March ye 12.

There came a young girl about 13 years of age, whose name was Alice Phenix, who came to this town to a shop for half a stone of towe for her master, being an apprentice to her master, Wm. Ward, of the Peak Forest. She went from this towne in the evening, and called at Peter Down's house, who liv'd then at Laneside. They sent her away in good time to have gone home. She turned againe, and was found at the house when they were going to bed. Peter called her in and sent her to bed with his daughter. Next morning, calling her up very soon, he sent her away, but as they were going to plough found her again, and his son did chide her very ill, and she deemed then to make best haste home; but sitting down betwixt two ruts in George Bowden's part on Paislow, sat there that day and next, and Friday, Saturday, Sunday, and Monday till noon. Two of which days, the 15th and 16th, was the most severe snowing and driving that had been seen in the memory of man. This girl was found about one o'clock on Monday, by William Jackson, of Sparrowpit, and William Longden, her neighbour in the forest. They carried her to the same house back again, to Peter Downe's house; and after she had got some refreshment, a little warm milk, could warm herself at the fire afterwards, and could turn her and rub her legs with her hands, and after was carried to her master's house that night, and is now (March 25th, 1717) quite well, but a little stiff in her limbs. This is the Lord's doings and will be marvellous in future generations. She had no meat these five days, but was very thirsty and slept much.

Location: SK23 0EN

Above: Church Brow, Chapel-en-le-Frith.

Below left: Market Place in the small Peak District town of Chapel-en-le-Frith.

Below right: Parish Church of St Thomas à Becket.

Halter Devil Chapel

Francis Brown lived and worked on his farm near to the tiny village of Mugginton. There had been farms in the area since before the Normans, and the village itself is thought to have taken its name from an unknown Saxon farmer, and means 'the farm of Mugga or Mogga'.

Brown, a much-troubled man, actually farmed at nearby Hulland Ward. It was believed, although not proven, that he had misappropriated some public funds and, partly in guilt and partly for total enjoyment, had taken to heavy drinking. One stormy night in 1723 he decided to go out into one of his fields to prepare his horse for an early start the following morning, as he had to collect a load of coal from Denby village, a journey of around 10 miles. Sensing his intention, Brown's long-suffering wife implored him not to go out on such a stormy night, but to wait until the morning. Brown's response was to go out into the fields anyway, as, by this time of the night, he was well under the influence of the demon drink and in a state of complete intoxication.

For some considerable time, holding the halter, he chased around after the horse in his inebriated state but couldn't seem to catch the animal. Then, feeling angry and frustrated, he shouted at the top of his voice, 'Ride I will if I have to

Halter Devil Chapel adjoined to the farmhouse.

Halter Devil Chapel.

halter the Devil.' Immediately, there was a flash of lightening and, all of a sudden, the horse was nowhere to be seen. Instead, Brown found, much to his surprise, that in his drunken state he had placed the halter around the neck of one of his black-horned cows. He viewed this single ill-considered act as being a direct encounter with the Devil himself, which quickly brought him back to his senses, and there, in the middle of the field, he reflected on his riotous living and the squandering of the money he had taken. He resolved from thereon in not only to live a sober life, but to become a truly reformed character. As a testament of his remorse and repentance he had built, within a matter of months, a chapel which adjoined the farmhouse where he and his family could worship. A plaque on one of the walls of the chapel proudly proclaimed, 'Francis Brown in his old age, did build him here an hermitage in 1723.' Directly below the plaque a mischievous note proclaimed, 'Who being old and full of evil once on a time haltered the Devil.'

The chapel itself has often been utilised as a dairy, but has now reverted to its original purpose.

Location: DE56 2LZ

Marshall Howe of Eyam

When the plague visited the tiny village of Eyam in 1665, villagers followed the advice of the vicar, Revd William Mompesson, and voluntarily isolated the village, even though this meant certain death for a large number of them. However, the coming of the pestilence also presented unforeseen opportunities for others, such as Marshall Howe, a local lead miner who lived in the village. Because of the distemper's unprecedented virulence, and also the fear of the contagion spreading, people were reluctant and disinclined to bury their dead. It was at this time that Marshall Howe took it upon himself to act as self-appointed sextant. Howe was not afraid of catching the disease himself, as he had suffered and survived the plague some while ago, and thus considered himself to be immune from further attacks. So, when people were exhorted to bury their own dead in their own land, Howe willingly offered his services.

It was soon voiced abroad that Howe was ready and able to bury the dead, even though, throughout the whole period, his wife pleaded with him to cease his perilous avocation. But the rewards were too great for him to resist. His preferred method of disposal was to make an initial assessment of the spoils he might gain from his labours, and then, having made his assessment, he would dig a shallow grave before tying a length of rope around the foot or neck of the corpse – in that way he didn't have to touch it when dragging it to the newly dug grave. Having finished his labours for the day, he would collect his rewards and then repair to the local hostelry, where he would boast to the assembled persons by declaring that 'He had pinners and napkins sufficient to kindle his pipe with while he lived.'

Howe's labours continued for many months, and during that time he disposed of several putrid and rotting plague-ridden bodies. On one occasion however, Howe was called to the home of a recently deceased person, a certain Edward Unwin. Following his usual practice, Howe first dug a shallow grave on Unwin's land, and then proceeded up the stairs to bring the, still warm, corpse down. Halfway down the stairs, a loud cry emanated from the corpse, followed by the cry, 'I want a posset.' It was at this point that Howe realised the 'corpse' was still alive! He immediately dropped the body from where it had been draped around his shoulders and swiftly departed the homestead. Receiving his posset some little while later, Edward Unwin recovered and went on to live to a ripe old age.

This event did not deter Howe from his chosen calling, that is until his own wife, Joan, was taken with the distemper. It was only at that time, when Howe saw the telltale buboes appear on her bosom, that he became painfully aware that he might have inadvertently brought the pestilence across his own threshold. After a short illness Joan Howe died on the morning of Monday 27 August 1666.

Right: Looking up Tideswell Lane towards Marshall Howe's House.

Below: Marshall Howe's House.

The Parish Church of St Lawrence, Eyam.

Howe buried her with a degree of dignity and circumspection which he had not previously demonstrated at other burials. But, more tragedy was to befall the now hapless Howe. On his return home, he found that his only son, William, was now exhibiting the first manifestations of the plague. William fought the deadly disease for three long fever-ridden days. The inevitable end came on Thursday 30 August 1666, and he was buried alongside the grave of his mother. Following the deaths of his wife and son, Howe buried many more people in the parish before the distemper finally departed, but with a little more care than he had previously shown.

Marshall Howe continued to live in the parish for many years after the plague had departed, and was laid to rest on 20 April 1698. For some generations after the plague, parents in Eyam would threaten to send for Marshall Howe if their children misbehaved.

Location: S32 5RD

Disaster at the Red Soil Mine

During the eighteenth century, lead mining, together with agriculture, accounted for much of the county's economic well-being, and the Magpie Mine, some 3 miles from Bakewell, was one of the most heavily worked. There are records relating to the mine dated as early as 1740, but the workings are, in all probability, much older. At the height of the mines' productivity, there were three separate mines working the Magpie vein, the Bole vein and the Butts vein: the Red Soil Mine, the Maypitts Mine and the Magpie Mine. Because of the close proximity of the veins, there was often tension and even skirmishes between the miners.

Many problems were encountered at the mines, such as the ingress of water, as this meant constant pumping out – a costly operation. Whenever the price of lead dropped, mining became unprofitable. But, more problematic, was the friction between miners when working veins crossed each other – the Magpie Mine and the Red Soil Mine both worked veins close to one another.

Miners often lit fires underground, as, by heating the working face and then cooling it with water, it made the lead more brittle and easier to extract; it also had the effect of smoking out the rival company's miners. The dispute between the Magpie Mine and its close neighbour the Red Soil Mine as to who owned a particular seam of lead ore started as early as 1824 and was set to continue for at least another ten years. The antagonism between the respective mines' workers continued unabated, until ultimately, on Monday 2 September 1833, three Red Soil Mine workers were found dead, presumably having suffocated. Although there was a noxious smell coming from the mine, the miners were allowed to make their descent. A number of the men felt as though they were suffocating. Two men turned back in order to raise an alarm. Eight men were rescued alive, but the other three, Isaac Bagshaw, Francis Taylor and Thomas Wager, did not survive. Further oral evidence suggested that Wager had lost his life in attempting to save Bagshaw and Taylor.

Countryside around Red Soil Mine.

Remains of Magpie Mine.

A post-mortem was conducted the following day. Initially it was assumed that the miners had died due to smoke inhalation from a fire set by Magpie miners using a mixture of straw, oil of coal, and sulphur. At the conclusion of the examination, a verdict of 'wilful murder' was returned against twenty-two of the Magpie miners, and seventeen were subsequently committed to the County Gaol to stand trial at the Lent Assizes at Derby on Wednesday 19 March 1834.

The trial of the miners began on Saturday 22 March 1834; the court sat from nine o'clock in the morning until almost eight o'clock in the evening and acquitted eight of the miners. The trial was adjourned until eight o'clock on the following Monday when the remaining miners were tried for murder. Much of the case hinged on whether any of the defendants were guilty of any offence whereby smoke, damp, or foul air was generated, which might have caused the death of the three Red Soil miners. It was difficult to ascertain exactly what had gone on underground, as the court only had the evidence of the miners themselves upon which to base their judgement. The court heard that death could have been caused by suffocation, but what was established was the fact that sulphur was not the cause of death. This was proved when the men who came out alive were examined; they were not exhibiting any symptoms of breathing sulphurous air. When the trial resumed, five of the defendants were acquitted on the direction of the judge.

During his summing up, which took almost four hours, the judge, for the benefit of the jury, differentiated between murder and manslaughter. Of the men that had previously been acquitted, the judge said that he could not ascertain whether those men had been in the mine at the time in question, and there were still questions remaining as to whether there was intent to kill the three men who had died, although the judge did acknowledge that there was an ongoing dispute between the mines' owners and the miners themselves. The jury then begged to retire, but returned to the court less than ten minutes later, finding all the prisoners 'not guilty'.

Many still believe that some of the wives of the 'murdered' miners cursed the mine, and it was certainly true that, from that time onwards, the mine's output and profitability began a steady decline. There are also those who hold to the belief that the mineshaft is haunted by the spirits of the three men who died in 1833.

Location: DE45 1QU

The Small-tooth Dog of Norton

The tale of the Small-toothed Dog was told in the village of Norton. A much-travelled merchant lived in the village and on one of his journeys he was attacked by thieves. The thieves were intent on taking his money, but a large dog came to his rescue. Remarkably, when the dog had driven the thieves off, he insisted that the merchant went back to his house, where he nursed him until he returned to full health. Just before the merchant was about to return home, he offered to give the dog his most precious possession as a token of his gratitude for all that he had done for him.

The merchant offered him a fish that could speak twelve languages, but the dog declined the offer. Next he was offered a goose that laid golden eggs, but once again the dog declined. Finally, the merchant offered the dog a mirror in which it was possible to see what anybody was thinking about. Unbelievably, the dog once again refused the merchant's offer. In desperation, the merchant asked what exactly the dog would like as a fitting reward. The dog replied that he would like the merchant's daughter to come to his house. The merchant was not overjoyed with this answer, but he had made a promise, so, he told the dog that he could come and fetch his daughter after he had been at home for a week. At the end of the week the dog came to the merchant's house to fetch his daughter, and a little while later she came out of the house dressed for the journey. Although the dog's house was some distance away, they soon reached their destination with the young girl on the dog's back. Everything went well for the first week, but then the girl became homesick. When the dog asked why she was feeling so low, she simply replied that she wanted to go home. The dog agreed to take her but, just before they were about to leave, he asked her what she called him. Her answer, that he was 'A great, foul, small-tooth dog', did not please him, and he refused to take her to see her father. The girl cried so pitifully that the dog promised again to take her home. Once again, the dog asked her what she called him. This time she answered, 'Your name is Sweet-as-a-honeycomb.' The dog allowed the girl to jump on his back and they went on their way. When they had travelled some 40 miles they reached a stile. Before climbing over, the dog asked her once again what she called him. She replied, 'A great, foul, small-tooth dog.' The dog immediately turned right around and galloped back to his own house with the girl on his back. After another week, the girl was weeping so bitterly that the dog once again promised to take her to her father's house. When they reached the stile the dog stopped and asked her what she called him. 'Sweet-as-a-honeycomb,' she replied. They carried on until they came to another stile. At this point the dog asked her once again what

Parish Church of St James the Great, Norton.

she called him. Being nearer home and feeling more confident, she answered, 'A great, foul, small-tooth dog."' Totally outraged, the dog turned around and galloped back home.

Another week passed, and, following more tears, the dog once again promised to take her back to her father's house. So she mounted upon his back, and when they arrived at the first stile the dog asked the same question and, being on her best behaviour, she replied 'Sweet-as-a-honeycomb.' When they arrived at the door of the merchant's house the dog again asked what he was called. She was about to say, 'A great...', but when she saw the dog turning to leave, she thought of the kindness that she had been shown over the last few weeks, and said 'Sweeter-than-a-honeycomb.' Astonishingly, the dog then stood up on his hind legs, pulled off his dog's head and tossed it high in the air. Stood in front of her was a most handsome man. They were married, and lived happily ever after.

Location: S8 8JQ

The Remarkable Phoebe Bown

Church registers record that Samuel Bown, a carpenter, married Phoebe, the daughter of John Mather, at St Giles' Church, Matlock, on 28 April 1756. Their youngest child was named Phoebe after her mother. She was baptized on 24 November 1771.

As she grew up it was clear that young Phoebe was different and, not only was she different but was particularly proud to be so. She even dressed in what was considered at the time to be men's clothing, wearing a heavy overcoat and a tall hat, under which she had a handkerchief, which was tied under her chin. Her diet too was different from most of her contemporaries; throughout her life she refrained from drinking very much alcohol and didn't eat beef or pork, and very little mutton, but she did drink lots of milk.

Her chosen work was often characterised as being men's work; she demonstrated skills as a carpenter and a mason, and was also skilled in other farm occupations such as sowing, mowing and reaping; indeed, the list of Phoebe Bown's skills and accomplishments cannot be overestimated. Although diminutive in stature she was more than able to thatch a barn or, single-handedly, drive a team behind a plough. Also, it was not unknown for her to walk over 40 miles in a single day, but much of her enjoyment came from breaking in horses, which she did for a guinea a week. She was a hostler, farrier and groom and always rode without a saddle. She was also, reputedly, the best judge of horses in the county, often being asked to make purchases for others at livestock markets and fairs.

However, there was a more cultured side of Phoebe Bown, and, when the mood took her, she could converse with authority on many different subjects and could often be heard quoting from Locke. She also amazed people when quoting correctly from memory lengthy passages from Milton, Shakespeare, and Pope.

Phoebe had a passionate love of music and was a versatile, if not particularly gifted, self-taught musician, playing violoncello, flute and harpsichord.

Matlock Derwent Bridge.

Above: Road into Matlock.

Left: River Derwent at Matlock.

She also supported the bass-viol in Matlock church. Although not being the most proficient of musicians, Phoebe never held back from questioning the proficiency of others; her views did not always meet with accord or approbation.

Constantly in fear of being robbed or accosted because of the social unrest at the time and the threat of riots, Phoebe always carried a weapon of some description on her person. She was also given to making bayonets, spears, and swords, which she then concealed in every conceivable hiding place in the house.

Sometime before her death, the curate of Matlock, Revd Gaunt, penned an epitaph which, by all accounts, pleased her:

Here lies romantic Phœbe,
Half Ganymede, half Hebe;
A maid of mutable condition,
A jockey, cowherd, and musician.

In her later years, much of her manual dexterity deserted her and she could no longer wield the tools of her chosen trades. This caused her to fall into poverty and she was reduced to relying on friends and neighbours to minister to her frugal needs. The Duke of Devonshire heard of her predicament and granted her an annuity of five shillings per week for life; she would not have to end her days in penury. The pension was administered by her relative, Lady Paxton, and paid to her by Mr Chinnery.

Phoebe appears to have had some sort of premonition that she would die on 4 May, and duly made herself a set of grave clothes in readiness. She did die in May 1854, but not on the 4th.

Location: DE4 3PS

Chesterfield's Crooked Spire

It is believed that Chesterfield's parish church was built during the period 1234 to 1360, although there remains some disagreement as to the exact dates. The church was built in local stone in a Decorated Gothic style and was dedicated to Saint Mary whilst, later on, it was dedicated to All Saints. Today, the parish church is known as St Mary and All Saints and is the largest parish church in the diocese of Derby.

Several theories have been forwarded as to why the spire became twisted. Some people believed that the twisting was due to the fact that many of the skilled craftsmen who would have been engaged in the building of the church and its spire had died during the Black Death, which was endemic at the time, and that unskilled labourers were employed who had neither the skills nor the knowledge to complete the project as originally envisaged.

Chesterfield Church.

Above left: Chesterfield's Crooked Spire.

Above right: The Parish Church of St Mary and All Saints, Chesterfield.

The truth is, however, very different from this. The spire was built using green, unseasoned timber, which was more malleable than the much-harder seasoned timber, which often proved too difficult to work with given the unsophisticated hand tools available at the time. The frame was then clad with wooden shingles, but when the shingles needed to be replaced lead was chosen as a longer-lasting material. Also, lead was mined extensively in the Peak District, so it was a viable alternative. Unfortunately, the weight of the lead tiles, approximately 32 tons, on the wooden framework caused problems, as the frame had not been designed to take such a weight. It was also noted that the lead on the south side of the spire was exposed to the sun for most of the day, which caused the lead to expand, but the tiles on the north-facing side of the spire were not subjected to such heat and did not expand or contract in a similar manner to the south-facing tiles. Over a long period, the uneven expansion and contraction inevitably caused the spire to twist. Architects also pointed to the fact that in the original construction there was little need for cross bracing, but, when the lead tiles replaced the wooden shingles, cross bracing became more important, but no further strengthening was made.

There is much folklore concerning the twisted spire, with many of the tales involving the Devil. One of the more popular tales is that an evil wizard tricked a blacksmith, working over in Bolsover, into shoeing the Devil. As soon as the blacksmith realised who he was working for, he started to shake in terror, and in so doing he accidentally knocked a nail into the more tender underpart of the Devil's foot. Now in considerable pain, the Devil took flight and headed off in the direction of Sheffield. As he skimmed over the parish church at Chesterfield, he lashed out in pain and anger and inadvertently caught the spire, twisting it out of shape. Another version declares that one day, whilst the Devil was sat resting on top of the spire with his tail wrapped around it, the people of the town took offence and started to ring the church bells. The sudden deafening sounds alarmed the Devil so much that he promptly jumped off, but, because his tail was still wrapped around it, his leaving caused the spire to twist. There is another tale which suggests that on his way to Sheffield he stopped and took some rest on top of the spire, but, smelling incense, he sneezed, and it was the violence of the sneeze that caused the spire to twist. The most risqué tale casts aspersions on the women of Chesterfield. The story, as related at the time, alleges that as the Devil was resting on the spire, he thought that he saw a virgin going into the church to get married. He was so amazed by the sight that he twisted around to try and see such a wonder, but, as he turned, his tail became stuck, and with it twisted the spire. The tale goes on to allege that if another virgin gets married in the church, then the spire will revert to its original shape.

Location: S40 1XJ

The Pentrich Rising

At the end of the French Wars, it was clear that England was in the throes of political, economic and social turmoil, with returning soldiers and sailors unable to secure gainful employment. A series of poor harvests only served to exacerbate the problem. Upwards of one third of the working population was unemployed during the harshest times of the depression. Another element that didn't help the dire situation was the abolition of income tax in 1816, which favoured the wealthy and led to the government having to borrow even more money, which, in turn, led to more indirect taxes, rising prices and more unemployment. This situation was set against a backdrop of the massive national debt, which was largely due to the government having to borrow a large amount of money in order to finance the war with France.

The country was undergoing rapid change during this time, with many activists pressing for political reform. There was definitely a widely held view that rebellion was in the air. In 1817 the men of the village of Pentrich, on the Derbyshire-Nottinghamshire border, having formed themselves into what could be loosely termed an armed force, were intent on marching to Nottingham, where they were expecting to join with other similarly minded men in an attempt to overthrow the government in power.

Pentrich Village Hall, formerly the school and, before that, the site of Thomas Bacon's cottage.

Revolution House at Whittington.

In an effort to combat this growing tide of discontent and social unrest, the Home Secretary, Lord Sidmouth, had taken the precaution of ensuring that he had spies embedded into various revolutionary groups throughout the country. The main aim was to garner information regarding any pockets of unrest and, in so doing, anticipate any possible uprisings. One of Sidmouth's most trusted informants was William Richards, better known as 'Oliver the Spy'. The brief he had been given from Sidmouth was to gain the confidence of the ringleaders and inform the government of any significant developments. Oliver attended many meetings, predominantly in the north of England. It was on one his foray's north that he met with Thomas Bacon of Pentrich, and it was he who, unwittingly, became Oliver's main source of information. Having gained Bacon's confidence, he was able to inform Sidmouth of the latest developments: the Pentrich Rising had been anticipated.

The three leaders of the Pentrich Rising were Jeremiah Brandreth, known as the Nottingham Captain, an unemployed stocking knitter; Isaac Ludlam, a bankrupt farmer; and William Turner, a stonemason and ex-soldier. On Sunday 8 June 1817, Brandreth addressed a crowded meeting in the White Horse Inn in Pentrich. He delivered a truly inspiring oration, telling the assembled group that the time for action had come, urging every man present to 'turn out and fight for bread'. When calling on the men to march to Nottingham, he offered them many inducements including bread, beef and ale. Much of what had been said that night was following Oliver's suggestion to Thomas Bacon that the only way to effect change was by using physical force. He convinced the leaders that 'half the country is in an organised state ... particularly in the manufacturing districts'.

The following night, a small group of around 300 men set off from Hunt's Barn in Garner's Lane, South Wingfield, to march to Nottingham where they believed they were to join with groups of other men fighting for the same cause.

The Dog Inn, known as The Spaniel Dog, at the time of the revolution.

The men, mostly quarrymen, ironworkers and stockingers, armed with scythes and pikes, were intent of securing better living conditions for the working classes.

Leaving in the pouring rain on a cold and dark night, Brandreth led his bedraggled men towards Nottingham, encouraging them to sing to keep up their morale. When the marchers reached Giltbrook in the early hours of the morning they were confronted by a detachment of twenty fully armed soldiers of the 15th Light Dragoons accompanied by two magistrates. The men fled, but were soon captured and taken into custody.

Following the trial at Derby, Brandreth, Turner and Ludlam were sentenced to death for treason. They were hanged on 7 November 1817, their heads severed before they were taken to St Werburgh's Church on Friargate for burial. Fourteen of the other men were sentenced to transportation, and another twenty were given custodial sentences.

There was somewhat of a dilemma concerning the trial of Bacon, as it was from him that Oliver had obtained much of his information. But, if Bacon was to be put on trial, it would necessarily mean that Oliver's name would be mentioned in court and thus, the government's case would be compromised. Instead, it was suggested that Brandreth rather than Bacon was the leading radical in Pentrich. Bacon was offered plea bargaining whereby in return for him pleading guilty to a lesser charge, he would be spared the gallows.

Location: DE5 3RR

The Gabriel Hound

Some distance between Hathersage and Eyam there is a deep dell known as the Clough. There are only a few dwelling houses in this area, many of them inhabited by families that have lived there for many generations. In one such dwelling there lived an old man of eighty named Bowman. Many years since, he and his sister Mary had been the only children of their doting parents. Mary Bowman, a few years younger than her brother, was regarded as being extremely beautiful. She was very tall and grand in shape and bearing; her eyes and hair were dark brown, almost black, and she had a high colour in her cheeks. When she was just eighteen years of age she fell in love with a man named Birch, the son of a local farmer. Her father, although not too pleased with the liaison, did not forbid it, but indicated to his daughter that he 'would rather graft on a better stock'. Nonetheless, the couple continued in their relationship and, at length, announced the date of their wedding. However, some weeks before the wedding, Mary's father received a letter from his landlord informing him that one of his relatives would be visiting the area and wished to go shooting on the moor. The letter went on to ask Mr Bowman if his relative could stay in their farmhouse during his visit, and asked if he, Mr Bowman, would accompany his relative during his week's shooting. Mr Bowman felt very honoured with this proposal and immediately informed his landlord that he and his family would be only too pleased to receive his relative.

A week or two later a charming young man named Galliard arrived at the farm. He was immediately smitten by the beauty of Bowman's daughter. He neglected the sport on the moors and turned his attentions to the young Mary Bowman. He even extended his stay, openly declaring his honourable intentions for the charming young woman. She however remained faithful in her feelings towards young Birch. Both her mother and father pleaded with her to accept the offer that the young man was making, but Mary would not hear of it. She also knew that she was at a complete loss as to how she could satisfactorily resolve the situation; she turned to her brother for help.

A plan was concocted by Mary, her brother, and Birch whereby she would feign a sudden and life-threatening illness. She took an emetic which made her look pale and become a little feverish. After suffering from this illness for some days she appeared to take a turn for the worse. Her parents and Galliard became more worried and began to wonder if the illness would prove to be terminal. Then, one evening when Bowman, his wife and Galliard were stood at Mary's bedside, all three of them heard a piercing yelping coming from outside of the house. Immediately, Mrs Bowman flinched and shouted, 'My God, 'tis the Gabriel

Looking towards the Clough.

hound – death is in our dwelling.' They heard the piercing cry twice more and knew that Mary's fate was sealed.

Galliard was deeply perplexed and didn't know what to do; he left the farm the following morning, never to return. Bowman accompanied him for the first few miles of his journey, but on his return his wife exclaimed, 'She is gone, my Mary!' Bowman took it to mean that his daughter had died during his absence, but that wasn't the case. His wife informed him that shortly after he had left with Galliard, Mary had disappeared and could not be found anywhere. It was assumed that she had eloped with Birch, that her illness had been feigned and that the yelping of the Gabriel hound had been performed by Birch and her brother.

Location: S32 1BR

The Shoemaker from Dore

There once lived in the village of Dore a poor shoemaker who couldn't make or sell enough shoes to keep his wife, himself and his family. He found it very difficult to live with this situation. Then, one day when he came downstairs one morning, he found that a piece of leather that he had cut out the previous day had already been made up into a pair of shoes. The shoemaker recognised that the beautiful shoes had been made by a true craftsman. The shoes were sold as soon as one of his customers saw them. The shoemaker's first reaction was to go out and buy more leather, enough to make at least two pairs of shoes. The shoemaker went to bed that night a happy man, but mystified as to who had made the shoes he had sold that day.

The following morning, when he went down to his workshop, he found that the leather that he had bought had now been made into two beautiful pairs of shoes, but he was still no wiser as to who had made them – but that didn't deter him from selling them!

As the shoemaker was curious as to who was making the shoes for him, he told his wife that he would stay up all night to see exactly what was happening. It surprised him when he found that it was none other than Hobthrust (Hob Thrust) who was

Christ Church, Dore.

Vicarage Lane, Dore.

Village Green, Dore.

making the shoes. All he knew about Hobthrust was that he was a brownie-like fairy who was very different from other fairies, as he always carried an iron pot containing thumb bones of children mixed with sand. But the shoemaker wasn't too bothered about all of the stories that he'd heard about Hobthrust; his main concern was to find suitable places for the shoes as soon as they had been made. However, the shoes were being made so quickly that it wasn't very long before the whole of the shoemaker's workshop was filled with bespoke shoes of every style. In the end, in desperation, the shoemaker began to throw the newly crafted shoes out of the workshop window as soon as Hobthrust had made them.

It appeared that Hobthrust's night-time activities were not restricted to working at the shoemaker's workshop alone. Hobthrust was also known to have spent some time working at one of the local farms in Dore. One morning, when the farmer started on his day's work, he found that the hay upon a rough piece of stony ground had been newly mown. Similar events occurred over the next few nights, so, like the shoemaker, the farmer decided to stay up all night to see what was happening. He found, just like the farmer before him, that the work was being done by Hobthrust.

Location: S17 3GX

Rescued from a Living Tomb

In the winter of 1815, when working conditions were particularly perilous underground, John Frost, a young Wesleyan preacher, was employed in one of the mines at Hucklow. When the earth where he was working, effectively, caved-in, Frost had a miraculous escape. It was reported at the time that 'his voice was heard from beneath the ground in which he was entombed, and it was ascertained that his head and body remained unhurt, the principal weight having fallen upon and bruised his thighs and legs'.

As the rescue mission required great skill and knowledge, the most experienced miners were brought in to accomplish his release. When the situation was assessed, it appeared that a mass of earth was suspended over his head, where it hung like an avalanche ready at the slightest touch to fall and crush him to death. The miners, aware of the delicacy of the situation and the danger facing their colleague, were forced to proceed with infinite caution, which obviously meant that, by definition, it would be a lengthy process. The rescue operation was mounted on Monday, the day when the accident took place, and continued until the evening of the following Thursday, at which time they were rewarded by witnessing the complete success of their exertions, and the restoration of John Frost to his family.

Frost was extricated from his dreadful situation suffering only a few slight bruises and a broken leg, after having been buried for upwards of seventy-five

Above: Group of lead miners.

Right: Bradwell Wesleyan Chapel.

hours. During the protracted rescue bid he was sustained by water dripping from above, which he was able to catch.

Following his miraculous rescue Frost confirmed that, as a Wesleyan Methodist, his strong religious feeling had given him strength, and neither pain nor apprehension destroyed his composure. He further confirmed that during his temporary incarceration he had sung psalms and hymns.

John Frost lived to be an old man and continued to be a local preacher to the end of his days.

Another remarkable rescue was enacted many years later at the Black Engine Mine on Eyam Edge where, in 1879, Dennis Bagshaw of Hucklow was working when the roof fell in. Bagshaw's workmates were on the engine shaft side and could easily escape, but he was on the other side of the subsidence and his escape proved to be impossible. As had been the case with John Frost, the rescue attempt was fraught with difficulty and danger. The miners who were drawn from Hucklow, Tideswell, Bradwell, Eyam and other places tirelessly worked from Monday morning until the following Sunday at noon. The rescue work was extremely dangerous because of the foul air in the mine; at one point even the rescuers' candles would not light. However, ventilation in the mine was

Little Hucklow Primitive Methodist Chapel.

Village of Little Hucklow.

restored when a safety gate was opened. During the rescue operation many of the workmen remained on duty continuously, not even taking time out to change their clothes or cease work to eat, preferring food to be sent to the mine so that they could continue with their labours, and, just like John Frost's earlier experience, Bagshaw had been sustained throughout the whole of the rescue period by catching drops of water that had dripped from the roof. He had caught the drops in an improvised cup he'd made of clay.

After nearly a week of strenuous efforts his colleagues managed to open the living tomb of Dennis Bagshaw. He, like his rescuers, was completely exhausted after his horrendous ordeal.

After a prolonged period of rest and recuperation, Dennis Bagshaw retired to Hayfield where he spent the rest of his life.

Location: SK17 8RT

An Unusual Wedding

Sheldon, near Bakewell, is a typical White Peak village, developed in close proximity to many of the lead mines in the district. Located 1,000 feet above sea level, the village largely grew during the eighteenth century, which coincided with the height of the industry, but Sheldon is remembered for other reasons.

Church records in the parish show that in earlier times disparity of age was no bar to matrimony. In January 1753, it was recorded that a widow aged eighty was married to a young boy of just fourteen years of age. Owing to her infirmities, it appears that the bride had to be 'chaired' to the altar, although other accounts suggest that she walked up to the altar to make her marriage vows with the aid of crutches. Following the nuptials, she was preceded by a band and also had the rare honour of being accompanied by the Duke of Rutland's hornpipe player. At the festivities which took place immediately following the wedding, the bride insisted that her husband joined in and, although she was unable to dance, she did beat time to the music with her hands. Later, with her husband's help and the aid of her crutches, she was able to shuffle about the improvised dance floor.

Below left: Evidence of the farming community at Sheldon.

Below right: Looking towards the centre of Sheldon village.

The tiny village of Sheldon.

No expense had been spared and wedding guests were 'soundly drenched with showers of excellent liquor'. It was a wedding filled with much happiness. Unfortunately, the marriage was destined to come to an early end, as the bride was dead before the end of the month. The funeral sermon was preached by the same clergyman who had, only a matter of a few weeks previously, performed the nuptial ceremony.

Although small, Sheldon boasts another unique claim to fame. In 1601 a local resident watched a duck flying into a hollow tree. The strange thing was, the bird didn't appear to come out again! Before very long it became known as the Duck Tree. The tree was felled and sawn into planks some 300 years later, and it was at that point that carpenters noticed that each plank contained the life-sized outline of a duck. The mystery has never been explained.

Location: DE45 1QS

Bibliography

Addy, Sidney Oldall, *Household Tales and other Traditional Remains* (Sheffield: Pawson and Brailsford, 1895).

Andrews, William, *Curiosities of the Church* (London: Methuen & Co. Ltd, 1890).

Andrews, William, *Bygone Derbyshire* (London: Simpkin, Marshall, Hamilton, Kent, & Co. Ltd, 1892).

Andrews, William, *Curious Church Customs* (London: Simpkin, Marshall, Hamilton, Kent, & Co. Ltd, 1895).

Arnold-Bemrose, H. H., *Derbyshire* (London: Cambridge University Press, 1910).

Bowles, C. E. B., *Journal of the Derbyshire Archaeological and Natural History Society* (London: Bemrose & Sons Ltd, 1906).

Bradbury, Edward, *In the Derbyshire Highlands* (London: Bemrose & Sons, 1881).

Bryan Benjamin, *Matlock Manor and Parish* (London: Bemrose & Sons Ltd, 1903).

Cox, Revd J. Charles, *Memorials of Old Derbyshire* (London: Bemrose & Sons Ltd, 1907).

Cox, Revd J. Charles, *Three Centuries of Derbyshire Annals* (Bemrose & Sons Ltd, 1890).

Ditchfield, P. H., *Old English Customs* (London: George Redway, 1896).

European Architecture vol IV (Chicago: Smith & Packard, 1895).

Evans Seth, *Bradwell: Ancient & Modern* (Chesterfield: Broad Oak Press, 1912).

Firth, J. B., *Highways and Byways in Derbyshire* (London: Macmillan and Co. Ltd, 1908).

Hall, George, *The History of Chesterfield* (London: Whittaker & Co., 1839).

Hall, Dr Spencer T., *Days in Derbyshire* (London: Simpkin, Marshall, & Co., 1863).

Hope, Robert Charles, *The Holy Wells of England* (London: Elliot Stock, 1893).

Jennings, Louis J., *Rambles Among the Hills in the Peak of Derbyshire* (London: John Murray, 1880).

Kitchiner, William, *Receipts for Plain Cookery* (London: Houlston and Wright, 1869).

Millingen, J. G., *The History of Duelling* (London: Richard Bentley, 1841).

Palmer, F. P. and A. Crowquill, *The Wanderings of a Pen and Pencil* (London: Jeremiah How, 1846).

Paul, David, *Eyam: Plague Village* (Stroud: Amberley Publishing, 2012).

Pendleton, John, *A History of Derbyshire* (London: Elliot Stock, 1886).

Rhodes, E., *The Derbyshire Tourist* (London: Longman, Hurst, Rees, Orme, Brown, and Green, 1824).

Trueman, Edwin, *History of Ilkeston* (Ilkeston: John F. Walker, 1880).

Vaux, Revd J. Edward, *Church Folklore* (London: Griffith Farran & Co., 1894).

Ward, Revd R., *A Guide to the Peak of Derbyshire* (Birmingham: William Ward).

Wood, William, *Tales & Traditions of the High Peak (Derbyshire)* (Manchester: B. Gratton, 1903).

About the Author

David Paul was born and brought up in Liverpool. Before entering the teaching profession, David served as an apprentice marine engineer with the Pacific Steam Navigation Company.

Since retiring, David has written a number of books on different aspects of the history of Derbyshire, Cheshire, Lancashire, Yorkshire, Shropshire and Liverpool.

Also by David Paul
Eyam: Plague Village
Historic Streets of Liverpool
Illustrated Tales of Cheshire
Illustrated Tales of Yorkshire
Illustrated Tales of Shropshire
Illustrated Tales of Lancashire
Speke to Me
Around Speke Through Time
Woolton Through Time
Anfield Voices